Designed by Flowerpot Press
www.FlowerpotPress.com
CHC-0909-0623
ISBN: 978-1-4867-3109-1
Made in China/Fabriqué en Chine

Copyright © 2025 Flowerpot Press, a Division of Flowerpot Children's Press, Inc., Oakville, ON, Canada and Kamalu LLC, Franklin, TN, U.S.A. All rights reserved. Can you find the flowerpot? No part of this publication may be reproduced, stored in a retrieval system or transmitted, in any form or by any means, electronic, mechanical, photocopying, recording, optical scan, or otherwise, without the prior written permission of the copyright holder.

When spring arrives, people all around the world get ready for one very fun activity: gardening! One of the great things about gardening is that you can do it almost anywhere. You don't have to be a full-time farmer with a giant field to grow your own plants. No matter how small the space you are working with, or whether you are planting indoors or outdoors, you can grow something! You can learn all about soil, animals, plants, and your environment just from starting a garden of your very own.

Astronauts aboard the International Space Station are growing lettuce to study outer space gardening techniques.

The heaviest pumpkin ever grown was 2,323 pounds (1,054 kg)!

Some people play music for their plants to help them grow!

"Plant us! We promise you won't regret it."

HOW DO YOU CHOOSE A PLANT TO GROW IN YOUR GARDEN?

Do you wait for a plant to tap on your window and ask you to plant it?

Plants don't choose you, you choose your plants!

If you are a first-time gardener, it is best to start with plants that are easier to grow. A picky plant can be a headache for even the most knowledgeable gardeners!

What makes a plant easier to grow? There are two main things that can help or hurt a plant's growth: temperature and sunlight.

"I love all of this sunshine!"

Some plants are very particular about the temperature in their environment. Melons and eggplants will grow more slowly in temperatures around 40°F (4°C). They like to live in warmer climates.

Some plants need a lot of sunlight! Aloe vera, the plant known for soothing your skin if you get a sunburn, likes a lot of sunlight.

Some great beginner plants include: snap peas, sunflowers, carrots, cucumbers, and...

"It's pizza night, right?"

"We have plenty of tomatoes!"

Cherry tomatoes! These smaller tomatoes only require a pot and can be grown inside, unlike larger tomatoes that usually require more space and a tomato ladder for the vines to grow on.

Another easy and delicious plant to grow are potatoes. Have you ever had potatoes in your pantry that get too old and start sprouting weird spidery tendrils? Those are called eyes, and you can plant them to grow more potatoes. Potatoes take a while to grow, so they require gardeners to be very patient. But by harvest time, all the waiting will be worth it.

Sprouted potatoes

HOW DO YOU PLANT SEEDS?

Do your seeds plant themselves?

No way. So it's time to get your hands dirty!

It's important to have the right gear before you get started. One of the best things to have when you garden is a pair of gloves. Gloves protect your hands from getting dirty while you dig into the ground. Sometimes you need to use your hands to dig a little or to pat the dirt back into place.

Another tool that can be helpful in the garden are trowels. These tools are little hand shovels used to dig into the soil and form a spot where you can plant seeds.

gloves

trowels

gardening rake

gardening apron

Those aren't the only tools you can use. Garden aprons are perfect for keeping the dirt off your clothes. Watering cans, garden rakes, and a mini wheelbarrow can also come in handy when working in the garden.

Even with all these tools, you should know that when you are gardening, you are probably going to get a little dirty. That's part of the fun!

wheelbarrow

watering can

Once you have the right tools, you will need to know how to plant your seeds in the ground. Let's use lettuce as an example.

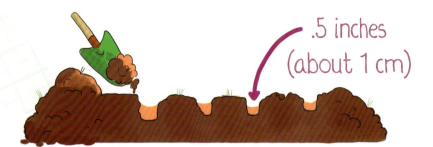

.5 inches (about 1 cm)

1. For lettuce, you will need to create a half-inch (about 1 cm) hole in the soil where you are planning to grow your lettuce.

2. Put your seeds in the hole. You will have a better chance of growing lettuce, and lots of other plants, if you plant multiple seeds in each hole.

3. After the seeds are in the hole, cover them with soil and gently pat the dirt.

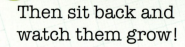

4. Use a watering can to give your seeds something to drink.

5. Then sit back and watch them grow!

However, not all plants are the same. Unlike lettuce, potatoes should be planted 6 inches (15.24 cm) deep into the soil. That is a lot deeper than the lettuce!

It is important to learn the specific things your plant likes. You can do this by checking the information on your seed packet, reading a book about your plant, or looking online.

Keep in mind that if you are planting multiple seeds in different holes, be sure to spread the holes apart. Plants need to have plenty of room to grow so they can get the full nutrients from the soil around them. A good rule of thumb is to dig your holes about 8 to 12 inches (20 to 30 cm) apart.

Can we look up how to plant tomatoes?

HOW DO PLANTS GROW?

Do they grow from seedlings into beautiful plants overnight?

Just like you, it takes time for a plant to grow. It doesn't just happen in one night! Also like you, plants grow in stages.

There are six different stages of growth for a plant. These stages are sprouting, seeding, vegetative, budding, flowering, and ripening.

The first stage is sprouting. It begins when you plant a seed into the ground. Each seed contains a small amount of nutrients that allow the seed to germinate. This is when the seed sprouts and begins growing into a plant.

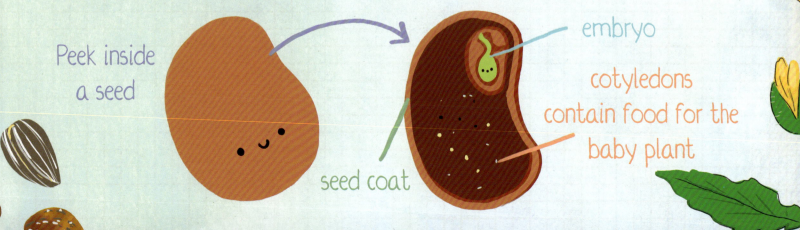

Peek inside a seed

embryo

cotyledons contain food for the baby plant

seed coat

The seed will not start to germinate until the conditions are just right. Giving your plant plenty of water and sunlight will help begin the process of germination.

SPROUTING

The second stage of plant growth is called seeding. This is when the roots grow and spread out in the soil. Roots are the part of the plant that anchors it into the ground, absorbs water and nutrients, and stores backup food for the plant.

SEEDING

Once the roots are strong enough, the plant enters the third stage of growth called the vegetative stage. This is when plants do the majority of their growing. The plant's goal at this point is to strengthen their stem, leaves, branches, and root system. By strengthening their stems, the plants are allowing more nutrients to flow through them, creating bigger fruits and vegetables.

The next stage is the budding phase. Rather than focusing on growing larger, the plant will focus on flowering and creating its fruit or vegetables. Plants can still grow larger during this stage but not as quickly as before.

After that comes the flowering phase. This is when pollination happens. Maybe you have seen a bee or another insect land on a plant and then zoom to another one. That insect is getting nutrients from the plant, but the plant is also getting something from the bug. Pollen gets caught on the bug and moved to another plant. The pollen then makes its way to a plant part called the pistil. This process creates seeds!

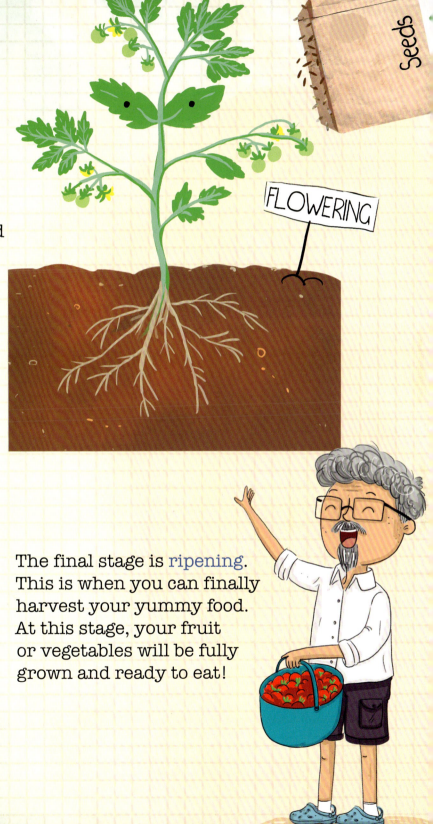

The final stage is ripening. This is when you can finally harvest your yummy food. At this stage, your fruit or vegetables will be fully grown and ready to eat!

HOW DO YOU KEEP YOUR PLANT HEALTHY?

Do you play rock and roll music to make it grow?

You don't need music, but there have been studies that show plants will grow away from a speaker playing rock and roll music!

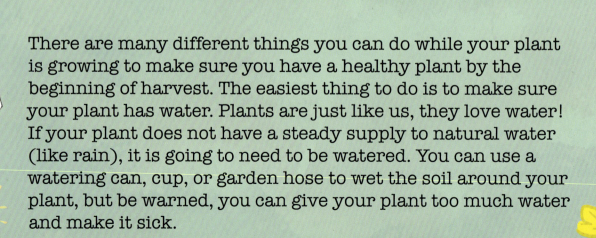

My data confirms country music is the best for plant growth.

There are many different things you can do while your plant is growing to make sure you have a healthy plant by the beginning of harvest. The easiest thing to do is to make sure your plant has water. Plants are just like us, they love water! If your plant does not have a steady supply to natural water (like rain), it is going to need to be watered. You can use a watering can, cup, or garden hose to wet the soil around your plant, but be warned, you can give your plant too much water and make it sick.

Slugs and snails can be major pests when it comes to keeping your plants healthy. Putting a copper ring at the base of the plant will keep the slugs and snails away, allowing your plant to grow.

Furry animals can cause problems too. Squirrels will sometimes try to dig up your seeds before they even grow. A natural way to deter these thieves is to spread hot pepper flakes around your garden. Squirrels have a strong sense of smell and taste. The pepper flakes irritate their senses which keeps them away.

While you are looking out for critters, keep an eye out for weeds. Unwanted grasses and other plants will try to grow around your garden. These weeds take away sunlight and nutrients from your plants. Use your gloves or garden tools to dig them out.

Make sure you spread pepper flakes after it rains because the water will wash them away.

HOW DO YOU GARDEN IF YOU DON'T HAVE A BACKYARD?

Do you make a portable garden in your house?

You can definitely have a garden inside, but you may not want to put it on wheels...

If you live somewhere without a backyard, you can get window boxes that hang right outside your window. These window boxes are perfect for apartments or tall buildings. Window boxes are usually smaller, so you may have better luck planting herbs, such as basil, or smaller fruits or vegetables, such as strawberries.

If you can't place a window box outside your window, growing plants indoors on the windowsill works just as well.

Some people may have the space, but don't have the soil. Do not fear! If you have a fence or wall, you can hang a garden. Much like outside of a window, these small gardens do not need a lot of space.

I'd like to plant some flowers, but I don't have enough space at home.

I have a solution!

Look at my homemade garden!

You can hang planters on a ladder like this!

If your backyard doesn't have soil, you can bring the soil to your backyard. Gardening soil is available at your local store and can be put in pots around your backyard.

Another cool option is a "no dig" garden. These gardens are planted in raised boxes that do not need to be dug into the ground. They can be as big or as small as you want and you can put them right where the sunlight hits in your backyard. These gardens are great because you have much more control over them than you would if you planted them in the ground.

HOW DOES A GARDEN HELP WITH THE ENVIRONMENT?

Is it because you can run your car on tomatoes?

Tomatoes are for pizza not trucks! A home garden, no matter how big or small, is a great way to help your local community and improve your environment.

One of the ways a home garden can help is by taking carbon dioxide out of the atmosphere. People, cars, and pets produce carbon dioxide and put it into the air. The good news is that plants need carbon dioxide in order to make food. So when more things are planted, you are helping reduce the amount of carbon dioxide in the air!

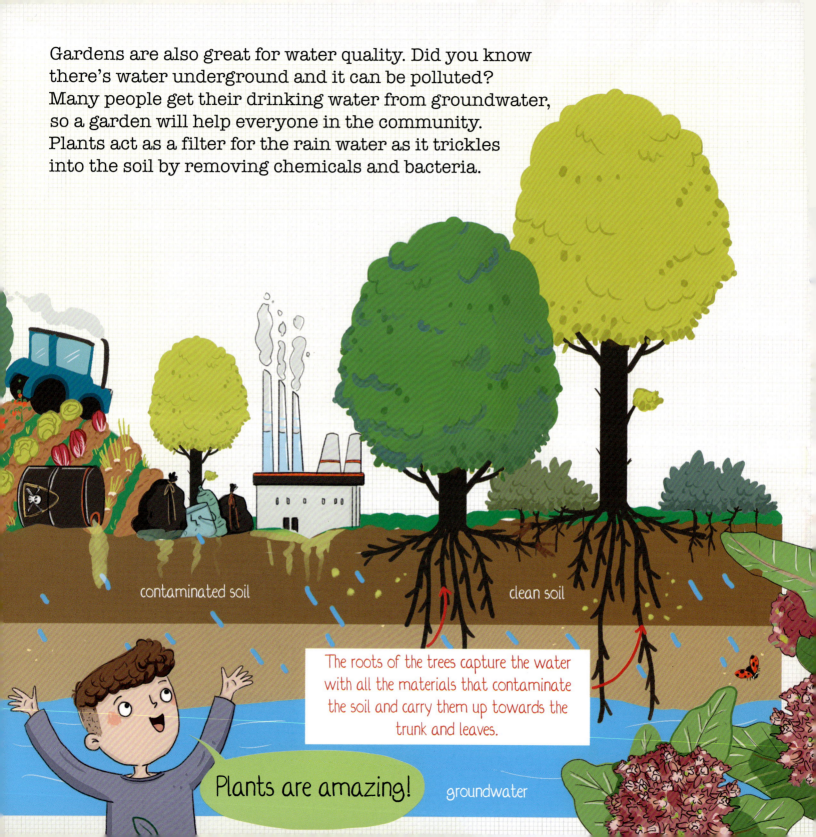

Gardens are also great for water quality. Did you know there's water underground and it can be polluted? Many people get their drinking water from groundwater, so a garden will help everyone in the community. Plants act as a filter for the rain water as it trickles into the soil by removing chemicals and bacteria.

contaminated soil

clean soil

The roots of the trees capture the water with all the materials that contaminate the soil and carry them up towards the trunk and leaves.

Plants are amazing!

groundwater

Another cool thing about having a garden is that you are helping your local wildlife. A good example of this is what your garden can do for Monarch butterflies. These butterflies make a yearly journey from the northern parts of North America to places such as Florida or Mexico. Because of humans building over their natural environment, Monarch butterflies are finding it harder and harder to get their favorite snack: milkweed. By planting this companion plant, not only will you see beautiful butterflies, but you can help make sure they have enough food for their journey.

A garden is just not about having food to eat (that is a big plus), but it can also mean a healthier lifestyle for you, your family, and your community!

Monarch butterfly

MAKE YOUR OWN WATERING CAN

Every gardener needs a watering can! Try making your very own at home.

What you need:
- Clean plastic milk jug or juice bottle
- Thumbtack or small nail
- Markers, paints, and glitter (optional)

Directions:

1. Remove any labels or stickers from the bottle so you have a clear surface to work with.

2. Ask an adult for help with this part! Use a thumbtack or small nail to poke 6 holes in the lid of the bottle.

3. Decorate your bottle using markers, paints, or even glitter!

4. Once you have finished decorating, remove the lid and fill the bottle with water. Make sure not to overfill it. You will need some space at the top to prevent spills. Be sure to screw the lid back onto the bottle securely to prevent leaks.

5. Now that you have your own homemade watering can, use it to keep your plants happy and healthy.

Dip your finger into the soil up to your second knuckle

dry finger

moist finger

THE FINGER DIP TEST

time for a drink

don't water

a happy, healthy plant

EGGSHELL HERB GARDEN

Try planting your very own herb garden using things you already have at home!

What you need:
- 12 eggs
- Egg carton
- Potting soil
- Herb seeds (basil, parsley, chives, or any others you like)
- Your homemade watering can or a spray bottle
- Spoon
- Paper (cut into 2-inch long rectangles)
- Toothpicks
- Tape
- Markers or colored pencils

Directions:

1. Carefully crack open the top of each egg near the pointed end. Try to crack the eggshell as neatly as possible so you have a large enough opening for planting. Empty the egg contents into a bowl and rinse the shells under running water. Allow them to dry completely. (The egg yolks can be used to make a yummy breakfast!)

2. Place the empty eggshells back into the egg carton. Fill each eggshell about three-quarters full with potting soil. Use a spoon to gently pack the soil down to create a firm base for planting.

3. Make a small hole in the center of each eggshell using your finger. Drop 2-3 herb seeds into each hole, then cover each one with a little bit of soil.

4. Water each one using your homemade watering can. Be careful not to overwater. Keep the soil moist but not soggy.

5. Label each eggshell with the name of the herb you planted by writing the name on a small slip of paper using markers or colored pencils. Attach the slip of paper to a toothpick with tape and place it in the carton next to the egg.

6. Find a sunny windowsill or another bright spot in your home to place the eggshell herb garden. Most herbs need plenty of sunlight to grow, so make sure they get at least 6-8 hours of sunlight each day.

7. Continue watering and caring for your herb garden. Watch as the seeds sprout and grow into healthy plants.

If your plants grow big enough, you can replant them in pots like this!

WHICH PLANTS GROW TOGETHER?

Ready to start planting your own garden? Use this handy guide to learn which plants can grow together.

IF YOU ARE PLANTING...

CARROTS

ALSO PLANT
- Beans
- Peas
- Lettuce
- Onion
- Tomatoes

POTATOES

ALSO PLANT
- Beans
- Corn
- Lettuce
- Spinach
- Radishes

TOMATOES

ALSO PLANT
- Basil
- Squash
- Cucumbers
- Carrots

STRAWBERRIES

ALSO PLANT
- Sage
- Squash
- Lettuce
- Chives
- Spinach
- Onions

ZUCCHINI

ALSO PLANT
- Corn
- Beans
- Peas
- Radishes

Remember to always follow the instructions on your seed packets.